Summer Bridge Readi
Grades K-1

Editors: Heather Canup, Julie Kirsch
Layout Design: Tiara Reynolds
Inside Illustrations: Magen Mitchell
Cover Design: Chasity Rice
Cover Illustration: Wayne Miller

ISBN 978-1-60022-443-0

Table of Contents

The *Summer Bridge Reading* series is designed to help children improve their reading skills during the summer months and between grades. *Summer Bridge Reading* includes several extra components to help make your child's study of reading easier and more inviting.

For example, an **Assessment** test has been included to help you determine your child's reading knowledge and what skills need improvement. Use this test, as well as the **Assessment Analysis**, as a diagnostic tool for those areas in which your child may need extra practice.

Furthermore, the **Incentive Contract** will motivate your child to complete the work in *Summer Bridge Reading*. Together, you and your child choose the reward for completing specific sections of the book. Check off the pages that your child has completed, and he or she will have a record of his or her accomplishment.

Examples are included for each new skill that your child will learn. The examples are located in blue boxes at the top of the pages. On each page, the directions refer to the example your child needs to complete a specific type of activity.

2

Summer Reading List

Banks, Kate
Max's Words

Beaumont, Karen
I Like Myself!

Brown, Margaret Wise
The Runaway Bunny

Cannon, Janell
Stellaluna

Carle, Eric
Pancakes, Pancakes!

Cronin, Doreen
Click, Clack, Moo: Cows That Type

dePaola, Tomie
The Legend of Old Befana

Donaldson, Julia
The Snail and the Whale

Ehlert, Lois
Snowballs

Ernst, Lisa Campbell
The Gingerbread Girl

Fox, Mem
A Particular Cow

Henkes, Kevin
Lilly's Big Day

Johnson, Stephen T.
My Little Yellow Taxi

Kates, Bobbi
We're Different, We're the Same

Lehman, Barbara
The Red Book

MacLachlan, Patricia
Three Names

Masurel, Claire
Two Homes

McClintock, Barbara
Adéle & Simon

McDonnell, Patrick
The Gift of Nothing

Meddaugh, Susan
Cinderella's Rat

Munsch, Robert
Love You Forever

Numeroff, Laura Joffe
If You Give a Mouse a Cookie

O'Connor, Jane
Fancy Nancy

Rathmann, Peggy
Ruby the Copycat

Reynolds, Peter H.
The Dot

Sendak, Maurice
In the Night Kitchen

Simon, Norma
All Kinds of Families

Small, David
George Washington's Cows

Seuss, Dr.
Oh, the Thinks You Can Think!

Viorst, Judith
Alexander and the Terrible, Horrible, No Good, Very Bad Day

Wiesner, David
Free Fall

Wood, Audrey
The Napping House

Ziefert, Harriet
A New Coat for Anna

3

Incentive Contract

List your agreed-upon incentive for each section below. Place an *X* after each completed exercise.

	Activity Title	X	My Incentive Is:
9	Sam and Max		
11	Great Groups!		
12	Meg the Vet		
14	It's Time for Titles		
15	The Best Title		
16	If I Had a Wish		
18	Mixed-Up Words		
19	Clues for You		
20	Pot of Gold		
22	In the Right Order		
23	All Mixed Up		
24	"What's for Lunch?"		
26	Super Synonyms		
27	Awesome Antonyms		
28	Sounds Good		

	Activity Title	X	My Incentive Is:
29	What's Big?		
31	Wheels		
32	Shh!		
34	Pack These Words for Camp		
35	The Odd Word Out		
36	Uncle Rich		
38	Chook, Chook		
39	Ants		
40	Finish the Words		
41	Jason and Lady		
42	This and That		
44	Questions		
46	The Birthday		
48	It's Time		
50	What a Character!		
51	What's That About?		

	Activity Title	X	My Incentive Is:
52	Mole		
54	Duke and Mule		
56	Long Vowel Sounds		
57	The Shipmate		
58	Dawn the Zookeeper		
60	It's Cold Outside		
62	The Zoo Crew		
64	Be a Word Detective		
65	Figuring It Out		
66	Troy and the Gold Coin		
68	Who Are the Characters?		
69	"Setting" the Stage		
70	Story Clues		
72	Our Tree House		
74	To the Moon		

	Activity Title	X	My Incentive Is:
75	Thunder and Lightning		
76	Where Do They Go?		
77	What Can You Find?		
78	World of Color		
80	Monkeying Around		
81	What Will Happen?		
82	Tanner and Andy's Clubhouse		
83	Worms in Dirt		
84	Could It Happen?		
86	Moving On		
87	Sisters		
88	What's the Title?		
89	Bats		
90	What's the Plot?		
91	A Day in the Garden		
92	Become a Writer		

Summer Bridge Reading RB-904091

Assessment Test

Circle the best answer for each question.

1. What is the middle vowel sound in the picture?
   A. a
   B. e
   C. i
   D. u

2. Choose the picture with the same vowel sound as *boat*.

   A.
   B.
   C.
   D.

3. Which word has the same sound as the underlined letters in the word h<u>at</u>?

   A. dog
   B. bird
   C. cat
   D. fish

4. Choose the word with the same meaning as *finish*.
   A. end
   B. begin
   C. wish
   D. find

5. What is the opposite of *clean*?
   A. nice
   B. dirty
   C. mean
   D. clear

6. Which of these events happened last?
   A. First, Billy took a bite.
   B. Then, Billy took a drink of water.
   C. Finally, Billy ate dessert.
   D. Next, Billy wiped his mouth.

5

Assessment Test

7. Write *C* in front of the sentence that tells the cause. Write *E* in front of the sentence that tells the effect.

_____ Maggie left her notebook on the school bus.

_____ Maggie couldn't study for her history test.

8. What word does not belong with the other words?

A. car   **B.** truck

C. school   **D.** van

Read the passage to answer questions 10–12.

Johnny Appleseed planted apple seeds for 49 years. He lived over 200 years ago. His real name was John Chapman. He walked barefoot around the country planting apple orchards. Some of the apple trees he planted still make apples.

9. Choose the title that tells what the story is about.

A. Making Apple Pie   **B.** Walking Barefoot

C. Johnny Appleseed   **D.** Eating an Apple

10. What is not a fact about Johnny Appleseed?

A. He planted apple seeds.

B. His real name was John Chapman.

C. He was a nice man.

D. He lived over 200 years ago.

11. Johnny Appleseed planted apple seeds for how many years?

A. 30   **B.** 49

C. 200   **D.** 2

12. The game was over. The team yelled, "Three cheers for Jim!" What probably happened?

A. Jim went to school.   **B.** Jim forgot the game.

C. Jim scored a goal.   **D.** The team ate dinner.

6

Assessment Test

13. Kevin likes to shop with his mom. Kevin pushes the cart. His mom picks food to put in the cart. Where is Kevin?

    A. a toy store   **B.** home

    C. a store that sells food   **D.** school

14. Follow the directions.

    A. Draw a square.

    B. Write *dog* above the square.

    C. Draw a circle inside the square.

Read the story to answer questions 16–18.

> Harry and Matt went outside to play baseball. They played in their backyard. Justin and Dan came to play, too. Matt threw the ball to Dan. Dan swung the bat. He missed the ball. Matt threw the ball again. Dan hit the ball hard. It flew over Matt's head. All the boys yelled, "Oh, no!" The ball was heading toward a window.

15. What do you think will happen?

    A. Dan will hit a home run.   **B.** Matt will catch the ball.

    C. Justin will throw the ball.   **D.** The ball will hit a window.

16. Where does this story take place?

    A. a baseball field   **B.** a house

    C. a backyard   **D.** a school

17. What is the main idea of the story?

    A. Dan hit the ball.

    B. Harry and Matt went outside to play baseball.

    C. The ball was heading toward the window.

    D. Justin and Dan came to play, too.

18. Which sentence is fantasy?

    A. Harry played baseball.   **B.** The boys played baseball.

    C. Matt threw the ball.   **D.** The ball screamed, "Oh, no!"

7

        Summer Bridge Reading RB-904091

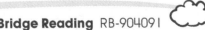

Assessment Analysis

After reviewing the assessment test, match the problems answered incorrectly to the corresponding activity pages. The child should spend extra time on those skills to strengthen his or her reading skills.

Number	Skill	Activity Page(s)
1.	long vowels	46–49, 52–57
2.	short vowels	9–10, 12–13, 16–17, 20–21, 24–25, 28–30
3.	consonant digraphs	32–33, 36–37, 40, 42–45
4.	synonyms	26
5.	antonyms	27
6.	sequencing	22–23
7.	cause and effect	60–61
8.	classification	11, 34–35, 76–77
9.	choosing titles	14–15
10.	fact or opinion	74–75
11.	reading for details	38–39
12.	inference	70–71
13.	context clues	18–19, 64–65
14.	following directions	82–83
15.	predicting outcomes	80–81
16.	setting	69
17.	main idea	31, 41, 51
18.	reality or fantasy	84–85

Summer Bridge Reading RB-904091

Sam and Max

Read the poem below.

Sam has a tan cat.

Max is Sam's cat.

Sam has a cap and a hat.

Sam has a bag and a bat.

Sam can tap the bat.

Max ran to the bag and sat.

Max naps and naps on the bag.

9

Sam and Max

After reading "Sam and Max," answer the following questions.

1. Write four words from the story that rhyme with *mat.*

_____ _____ _____ _____

2. What is the name of Sam's cat?_____

3. Name four other things listed in this story that Sam has.

_____ _____ _____ _____

4. Name another word that rhymes with

bag _____   tap _____   tan _____

5. Why do you think Max ran to the bag? _____

_____

6. Draw and label a picture of Sam and Max.

Summer Bridge Reading RB-904091

Great Groups!

Things can be grouped together if they are alike in some way.

Decide what the things in each picture have in common. Choose a group name from the word bank for each set of pictures. Then, write it on the line.

pets	shapes	things that go
food	farm animals	tools

1.

_____

2.

_____

3.

_____

4.

_____

5.

_____

6.

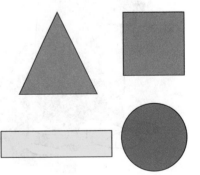

_____

Meg the Vet

Read the poem below.

Meg is a vet.

Vets help sick pets.

Vets help pets get well.

Some vets help big pets.

Some vets help little pets.

A vet can wrap a dog's leg.

A vet can mend a horse with a cut.

A vet can fix a cat with no pep.

A vet can help your pet, too.

Meg likes being a vet.

Meg the Vet

After reading "Meg the Vet," answer the following questions.

1. Which sentence tells the main idea?

    A. Pets get hurt a lot.
    B. Vets help pets.
    C. Cats have no pep.

2. Write a *T* for things that are true about vets. Write an *F* for things that are false.

    _____ Vets help pets.

    _____ A vet can help a horse.

    _____ Vets drive buses.

    _____ A vet can wrap a dog's leg.

    _____ Vets sell cars.

    _____ Vets fix bikes.

    _____ Vets mend horses with cuts.

3. How does the story say a vet can help a dog?

    A. mend a cat
    B. wrap a leg
    C. fix a cut

4. What is a vet?

    A. a pet doctor
    B. a people doctor
    C. a truck driver

5. Draw a line from each animal to its group.

Big pets

Little pets

gerbil
horse
hamster
cow
mouse
sheep

6. List three words with the short *e* sound from the poem.

_____

_____

_____

Summer Bridge Reading RB-904091

It's Time for Titles

The title of a picture or a story tells what it is about. Circle the best title for each picture.

1.

Fish in the Sea

My Pet Fish

2.

A Trip to the Moon

Planet Earth

3.

A Day at the Beach

Fun at the Pool

4.

A Bird Adventure

The Plane Ride

5.

I'm All Wet!

The Rainbow

6.

The Cat and Dog

The Cat Picture

Write your own title for the picture.

7.

_____

Summer Bridge Reading RB-904091

The Best Title

Read each title. Read each passage. Then, circle the best title for each passage.

1.   Ducks Are Made for Water

Ducks Fly South in the Fall

What can walk, swim, fly, and quack? Did you say a duck? Then, you are correct. Ducks like water. They live near ponds, lakes, streams, and the sea. They can swim better than they can walk. They have webbed feet. Their feet are wide and flat. There is skin between their toes.

2.   Why Ducks Wear Raincoats

How Ducks Stay Warm

Water can be very cold. Ducks have soft, white feathers next to their skin. These feathers are called *down*. Down holds warm air. On top of down, ducks have outer feathers. These feathers have a coat of oil. They work like a raincoat. The water runs off of them.

15

If I Had a Wish

Read the story below.

If I had a wish...
I'd wish for a fish.
I'd wish for a fish in a dish.

If I had a wish...
I'd wish for a ship.
I'd wish for a trip on a ship.

If I had a wish...
I'd wish for some chips.
I'd wish for some chips and some dip.

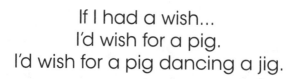

If I had a wish...
I'd wish for a pig.
I'd wish for a pig dancing a jig.

If you had a wish, what would you wish?

Summer Bridge Reading RB-904091

If I Had a Wish

After reading "If I Had a Wish," answer the following questions.

1. What could be a new title for this poem?

    A. Wishes

    B. Fish, Ships, and Pigs

    C. A Pig Can Jig

2. Draw a line between the rhyming words that were paired up in the story.

    fish   dip

    ship   jig

    chip   dish

    pig   trip

3. What does *jig* mean?

    A. a little dance

    B. a story

    C. a pet

4. Write *Y* if you think the wish could come true. Write *N* if you do not think the wish could come true.

    _____ a fish in a dish

    _____ a ship for a trip

    _____ some chips and some dip

    _____ a pig dancing a jig

5. What would you wish for?

_____

_____

_____

© Rainbow Bridge Publishing   Summer Bridge Reading RB-904091

Mixed-Up Words

Read each sentence. Look at the mixed-up word under the sentence. Put the letters in the correct order. Then, write the new word on the line.

1. Some dinosaurs hunted and ate _____.
   emat

2. Other dinosaurs ate _____.
   aplnst

3. Some dinosaurs had _____ on their backs.
   lsepat

4. Other dinosaurs had _____ on their heads.
   rhnos

5. Some dinosaurs had long _____.
   kcnes

6. Other dinosaurs had _____ arms.
   htrso

7. Baby dinosaurs hatched from _____.
   sgeg

Summer Bridge Reading RB-904091

Clues for You

Read each clue. Find the word in the list that makes sense in the blank. Then, write the word from the list in the puzzle.

Across

3. Bees _____ in hives.

4. A dog is one _____ of pet.

5. Ants live _____ the ground.

Down

1. Some birds _____ nests.

2. You can _____ your friend's hand.

4. Birds sit on eggs to _____ them warm.

Word List

keep

kind

live

hold

make

under

Summer Bridge Reading RB-904091

Pot of Gold

Read the story below.

One day, Josh went outside to play. He saw a big pot.
"Where is the gold?" Josh asked. "Pots always have gold."

Josh looked for the gold. He stomped his foot.
"Who has my gold?" he said.

Suddenly, a little man jumped out.
"You took my gold!" said Josh.
"No," said the little man. "You took my pot."
"This is your pot?" asked Josh.
"Yes," said the little man.

"I'm sorry. Here you go." Josh gave the little man his pot.
The little man gave Josh some gold.

20

Pot of Gold

After reading "Pot of Gold," answer the following questions.

1. Which sentence tells the main lesson of the story?
   A. If you find something, it belongs to you.
   B. Give things back to the person they belong to.
   C. Pots and gold always go together.

2. Write a *T* by each sentence that is true. Write an *F* by each sentence that is false.
   _____ Josh found a pot.
   _____ The pot belonged to Josh.
   _____ The little man gave Josh some gold.
   _____ Josh lost his gold.

3. Why did Josh stomp his foot?
   A. There was no gold in the pot.
   B. The pot had gold.
   C. The man had no gold.

4. Fill in the missing words from the story.

   pots   man   gold

   A. Josh gave the little

      _____ the pot.

   B. The little man gave Josh

      some _____.

   C. Josh thinks that

      _____ always
      have gold.

5. Why did the little man give Josh some gold?
   A. for being honest
   B. because he had extra
   C. because Josh asked for some

6. What is the opposite of *little*?
   A. big
   B. small
   C. nice

Summer Bridge Reading RB-904091

In the Right Order

These pictures are mixed up. Number the pictures in the order they would happen.

Extra!
After you number the pictures correctly, write a title for the story.

All Mixed Up

Sequencing means putting events from a story in the order they happened. A picture story can be put in order by looking at details in the pictures.

Number the pictures in the order they would happen.

1.

2.

3.

4.

Summer Bridge Reading RB-904091

"What's for Lunch?"

Read the story below.

"Would you like a hot dog on a bun?"
"No, thank you."

"Would you like a bunch of nuts?"
"No, thank you."

"Would you like a muffin with butter on it?"
"No, thank you."

"Would you like a cup of soup?"
"No, thank you."

"Then, what would you like for lunch?"
"Just some cud," said the cow.

"What's for Lunch?"

After reading "What's for Lunch?," answer the following questions.

1. In the story, who is being asked, "What would you like for lunch?"
   - **A.** a boy
   - **B.** a cow
   - **C.** a mother

2. Number what the cow was offered for lunch in order.
   _____ soup
   _____ nuts
   _____ hot dog on a bun
   _____ muffin

3. What did the cow want to eat for lunch?
   - **A.** a hot dog on a bun
   - **B.** some cud
   - **C.** a muffin with butter

4. Number the foods in the order that you would like to eat them. Start with your first choice.
   _____ hot dog
   _____ nuts
   _____ muffin
   _____ soup

5. What does *cud* mean?
   - **A.** a dessert
   - **B.** something cows chew
   - **C.** something to drink

25

© Rainbow Bridge Publishing

Summer Bridge Reading RB-904091

Super Synonyms

> **Synonyms** are words that have the same meaning.
> **Examples:**   small, little   big, huge

Read the word on each snowman. Choose a word in the word box that has the same meaning. Then, write the word under the snowman.

1.

hat

_____

2.

put

_____

choose	sleep
cap	place
run	keep
quick	kind

3.

fast

_____

4.

save

_____

5.

nice

_____

6.

rest

_____

7.

jog

_____

8.

pick

_____

26

Awesome Antonyms

> **Antonyms** are words that have opposite meanings.
> **Examples:**   fast, slow   good, bad

Draw a line from each word on the right to the word on the left with the opposite meaning.

1.	day		little
2.	long		night
3.	big		new
4.	hot		short
5.	old		under
6.	over		cold

Summer Bridge Reading RB-904091

Sounds Good

There are five main vowels: *a, e, i, o,* and *u.* The short vowel sounds are:
a as in *cat*   *e* as in *bed*   *i* as in *ship*   *o* as in *box*   *u* as in *tub*

Write the middle sound of each word using the correct vowel.

1.    c __ p

2.   d __ t

3.    l __ g

4.   f __ n

5.    m __ p

6.    l __ p s

7.    p __ g

8.   n __ t

9.    h __ t

10.    t r __ c k

Summer Bridge Reading RB-904091

What's Big?

Read the poem below.

"What's big?" asked the kid.

"An ant," buzzed the gnat.

"A rat," whispered the ant.

"A hen," squeaked the rat.

"A cat," clucked the hen.

"A dog," meowed the cat.

"A pig," barked the dog.

"A ram," oinked the pig.

"A yak," bleated the ram.

"The sun," bellowed the yak.

"Yes, the sun," said the kid.

"The sun is big."

What's Big?

After reading "What's Big?," answer the following questions.

1. Which sentence tells the main idea?
   A. *Big* is something bigger than you are.
   B. A gnat is the smallest animal.
   C. The sun is a big star.

2. Draw a line from each animal to its group.

   cat

   ant

   yak   Bigger than
                a dog
   pig

   rat   Smaller than
                a dog
   hen

   ram

3. Write a word from the poem on each line.

   short a word _____

   short e word _____

   short o word _____

   short i word _____

   short u word _____

4. Circle the words that were used in the poem to mean the same thing as the word *said*.

   whispered

   quacked

   jumped

   barked

   ran

   buzzed

Wheels

Read each passage. Read the choices. Circle the main idea for each passage.

1.   Wheels help us do work. They make it easy to move things. If cars, trucks, and trains didn't have wheels, they would not go. If a bike did not have wheels, it would not roll.

Trains have wheels.

Bikes can roll.

Wheels make things easy to move.

2.   A long time ago, men and women carried things on their backs. Donkeys and camels carried things in packs. Sometimes, they dragged things behind them. It was hard to move things without wheels. Men and women could not go far. Donkeys and camels could not carry very much.

Donkeys carry things in packs.

People had to move things without wheels.

People had to carry things on their backs.

Summer Bridge Reading RB-904091

Shh!

Read the poem below.

Shh! The baby's sleeping.
Please shut the door.

Shh! Your sister's napping.
Please don't shout.

Shh! Your dad is snoozing.
Please don't turn on the television.

Shh! Your grandpa's snoring.
Please don't shake your tambourine.

Shh! It's your bedtime.
Hush and shut your eyes.

Shh!

After reading "Shh!," answer the following questions.

1. Which sentence tells the main idea?
   - A. Children are too loud.
   - B. Moms like it quiet.
   - C. Be quiet when people are sleeping.

2. Who is "Shh!" probably being said to?
   - A. mom
   - B. child
   - C. dad

3. Who is probably saying "Shh!"?
   - A. Mom
   - B. Dad
   - C. teacher

4. Circle the people who are sleeping.

Mom	baby
sister	Dad
Grandma	Grandpa

5. What do you like to do to make noise?

   _____

   _____

   _____

   _____

   _____

6. Write an X by the words that mean the same as *sleeping*.

   _____ napping

   _____ snoozing

   _____ shouting

   _____ laughing

33

Pack These Words for Camp

Read each word in the box at the bottom of the page. Decide if it is something to eat, something to wear, or a place to live. Write it under the correct group name.

Something to Eat	Something to Wear	A Place to Live
_____	_____	_____
_____	_____	_____
_____	_____	_____
_____	_____	_____

Word List

shirt	pants	lodge	cheese	beans	tent
cave	cabin	bread	gloves	cap	apples

The Odd Word Out

Words that are alike in some way can be classified, or grouped, together.
Example: red   green   blue
These words can be grouped together as color words.

Read the words in each row. Cross out the word that does not belong with the other words.

Example: plate   ~~door~~   spoon   cup

1.   jump   skip   run   dog

2.   car   arms   legs   hands

3.   roof   window   toys   door

4.   den   girl   hive   cave

5.   pencil   crayon   marker   paper

6.   sit   sing   talk   yell

35

Uncle Rich

Read the poem below.

Our Uncle Rich always says,
"Children, choose one thing.
Anything you ask for,
that's the thing I'll bring."

Chad chose a choo choo train.
Chip chose a chair.
Chan chose a chopper toy
that flies in the air.

Chet chose some chocolate.
Chuck chose a chestnut.
Chester chose checkers,
his favorite game.

Uncle Rich brought each child
that one favorite thing.
But more than things,
it's joy that our favorite uncle brings.

36

Uncle Rich

After reading "Uncle Rich," answer the following questions.

1. Which sentence tells the main idea of the poem?

    A. Children like toys.
    B. Uncle Rich brings gifts.
    C. Uncle Rich has lots of money.

2. What does Uncle Rich bring that is better than things?

    A. anything
    B. chopper
    C. joy

3. What do the children get to choose?

    A. a chair
    B. one thing
    C. game

4. What does *joy* mean?

    A. money
    B. presents
    C. happiness

5. Group the following things.

    choo choo train   chair
    chopper toy   chocolate
    chestnut   checkers

Toy	Not a Toy

6. Draw a line between each pair of rhyming words.

thing   rain

chain   chair

air   bring

      Summer Bridge Reading RB-904091

Chook, Chook

Read the poem below.

Chook, chook, chook, chook, chook.
Good morning, Mrs. Hen.
How many chicks do you have?
Madam, I have ten.
Four of them are yellow,
Four of them are brown,
And two of them are speckled red,
The nicest in the town.

In this poem, Mrs. Hen proudly tells about her chicks. Fill in the graph below to show how many chicks she has of each color.

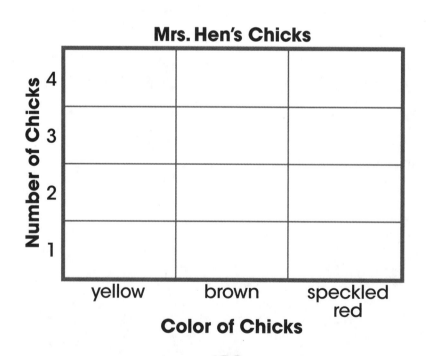

Ants

Read the passage below.

Ants are insects. They have three body parts. Ants also have six legs. They have antennae. Some ants are black and some are red. There are big ants and little ants.

Ants work hard. They work together. Each ant has a different job. Some ants carry sand. Some ants get food. The queen ant has many babies. Other ants take care of baby ants. Ants are very strong. They are hard workers.

Draw an ant. Use the details from the passage above.

Complete each sentence.

1. Ants have different _____ .

2. Some ants carry _____ .

3. The queen ant has many _____ .

4. Some ants take care of _____ .

© Rainbow Bridge Publishing   **Summer Bridge Reading** RB-904091

Finish the Words

> When the letters *ch*, *sh*, *th*, and *wh* come together at the beginning or the end of a word, they usually make one sound. They are called **consonant digraphs**.
> **Example:** *ch*ildren, *sh*op, *th*at, *wh*en

Add *ch*, *sh*, *th*, or *wh* to each word.

1.  __ __ i l d

2.  __ __ a l e

3.  c a t __ __

4.  __ __ i p

5.  w i __ __

6.  __ __ u m b

Find the words from above in the puzzle. The words will go across and down.

c	w	i	s	h	l	c
t	h	u	m	b	k	h
c	a	t	c	h	s	i
e	l	m	f	a	n	l
d	e	s	h	i	p	d

Summer Bridge Reading RB-904091

Jason and Lady

Read each paragraph. Circle the main idea.

1. Jason's dad gave him a new puppy. She was a beagle. She had brown, black, and white spotted fur. She was very cute. Jason named her Lady.

    A. Lady had a brown, black, and white spotted fur.

    B. Lady was cute.

    C. Jason had a new puppy.

2. Jason took care of Lady. He always fed her on time. He did not give her too much to eat. He took her outside. Sometimes, she made a mess. Jason had to clean it up. He did not mind. Jason liked his puppy.

    A. Jason took Lady outside.

    B. Jason took care of his puppy.

    C. Jason fed Lady.

41

This and That

Read the poem below.

This and that, in and out.
There are so many things to think about.

You can think about numbers.
You can think about math.
You can think where to go.
You can think of which path.

You can think about us.
You can think about them.
You can think about her.
You can think about him.

You can think about thimbles.
You can think about thread.
You can think out loud.
You can think in your head.

Just think of the things
you can think about.
Think!

This and That

After reading "This and That," answer the following questions.

1. Circle another title for this poem.
  A. Things to Think About
  B. Choosing the Right Path
  C. Thimbles and Thread

2. Name four things the poem says you can think about.

_____

_____

_____

_____

3. What else can you think about? Think!

_____

_____

_____

_____

_____

4. Draw a line between each pair of rhyming words.

math	about
out	head
thread	path

5. Write the words in the correct groups below.

this	math
that	think
there	things

th sound in *thin*	*th* sound in *then*
_____	_____
_____	_____
_____	_____

Questions

Read the poem below.

What should we do?

Watch a whale whack the wharf?

Whine about a wheel that's broken?

Whirl in circles on a whim?

Where should we go?

Where the wheat whips in the wind?

Where you can whistle while you work?

Where a whale whiffs the breeze?

When should we go?

When the man with white whiskers whispers, "Now"?

When the wind whistles which way to go?

When the wheel of the wagon has been fixed?

Summer Bridge Reading RB-904091

Questions

After reading "Questions," answer the following questions.

1. This is a nonsense poem. What does *nonsense* mean?

    A. does not rhyme

    B. does not make sense

    C. asks good questions

2. Number these activities in the order that you would most like to do them.

    _____ watch a whale

    _____ whine about a wheel

    _____ whirl in circles

3. Where would you go to see a whale whiff the breeze?

    A. the ocean

    B. the farm

    C. the zoo

4. What would you like to do?

_____

_____

_____

_____

_____

5. Circle all of the *wh* words in the poem. Write four of the *wh* words.

_____

_____

_____

_____

The Birthday

Read the story below.

It was Theresa's birthday. She invited Jay, Doris, Gayle, Jane, and Jake. Her friends came at the same time. They were ready for a day of play. They played a game of ball. They went for a hike on a trail. They raced back to eat cake. Theresa opened her gifts. Jay gave her a book. Doris gave her a fake snake. Gayle's gift was a toy monkey with a long tail. Jane gave her a DVD. Jake gave her a doll with a dress. Theresa had a fun birthday.

The Birthday

After reading "The Birthday," answer the following questions.

1. What is the main idea of the story?

    A. going for a hike

    B. Theresa's birthday party

    C. Theresa opening her gifts

2. Put the events from the story in order.

    _____ Jane gave Theresa a DVD.

    _____ They played a game of ball.

    _____ They raced back to eat cake.

    _____ Theresa opened her gifts.

3. What did Doris give Theresa?

    A. a fake snake

    B. a boat with a sail

    C. a monkey with a long tail

4. What presents would you like for your birthday?

_____

_____

_____

_____

5. Write each of the following long *a* words in the correct column.

cake	Gayle	train
sail	play	race
snake	day	Jay
same	tail	trail

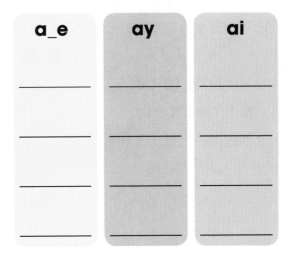

a_e	ay	ai
___	___	___
___	___	___
___	___	___
___	___	___

47

It's Time

Read the poem below.

It's time for what?
It's time for time!
Whatever is time for?

It's time to go to bed.
It's time to get up.
It's time to eat.

It's time to be good.
It's time to do your best.
It's time to learn.

It's time to go out.
It's time to come in.
It's time to be there.

It's time to grow up.
It's time to stay young.
Whatever your age, it's time.

It's your time to be.
It's my time for me.
Let's be friends, it's time.

Summer Bridge Reading RB-904091

It's Time

After reading "It's Time," answer the following questions.

1. Write three words that rhyme with *time*.

_____

_____

_____

2. The poem says, "It's time to eat." What time do you eat these meals?

breakfast _____

lunch_____

dinner_____

3. Write the antonym (opposite) of each of the following words. The words are in the poem if you need help.

in _____

stay _____

here_____

worst _____

old_____

you _____

down_____

stop_____

bad _____

Summer Bridge Reading RB-904091

What a Character!

A **character** shows her feelings and personality by what she says and does. This helps us understand a character.
Example: Christina is crying.
We know Christina is sad because she is crying.

Circle the word that tells about each character.

1. Ted likes to tell jokes.
He likes to make his
friends laugh.
Ted is a _____ person.

sad   funny   shy

2. Andy covers his eyes. He does
not like to watch lightning.
Andy is _____ .

proud   sad   afraid

3. Fran has many friends.
She likes to help her teacher.
Fran is a _____ person.

funny   nice   shy

4. Juan smiles after the race.
He wears his medal around
his neck. Juan is _____ .

silly   proud   shy

5. Mark starts to yawn.
He puts his head on his desk.
Mark is very _____.

tired   afraid   silly

6. Teri cannot find her
dog. She starts to cry.
Teri is _____.

happy   proud   sad

50

What's That About?

The **main idea** of a story is what the story is about. Read each story. Circle the sentence that tells the main idea.

1. George Washington was elected the first President of the United States of America. He was President from 1789–1797. He is often thought of as *The Father of His Country*.

   A. George Washington was the first President of the United States.

   B. George Washington was born in Virginia.

   C. George Washington went to school.

2. Abraham Lincoln had many different jobs. Abraham worked at a store. He also worked on riverboats. Later, he became a lawyer. He was elected the 16th President of the United States of America.

   A. Abraham Lincoln was born in a log cabin.

   B. Abraham Lincoln liked to read books.

   C. Abraham Lincoln had many different jobs.

3. Martin Luther King Jr. became the youngest person to win the Nobel Peace Prize in 1964. He won the award because he was a peacemaker. He hoped for nonviolence and equal treatment for everyone.

   A. Martin Luther King Jr. won the Nobel Peace Prize.

   B. Martin Luther King Jr. believed all people were born equal.

   C. We celebrate Martin Luther King Jr. Day in January.

Mole

Read the story below.

Mole was not bold. He was shy. He liked to hide in his hole by the road. Toad hopped by Mole's home. He saw a moat all around Mole's home. Toad poked at the moat. It was wet and cold. Toad called, "Hello, Mole! Do I see a moat?"

Mole froze in his hole. He had a boat to sail in his moat. He did not want old Toad to know. A wet toad would soak his boat. Again Toad shouted, "Hello! Do I see a boat for your moat?" Shy Mole wrote a note. He took a long pole. He poked the note up the hole. Toad read the note. It said, "Go away!" It was no joke. Toad sadly hopped down the road.

Next, Goat loped down the road. He saw Mole's home. He saw the moat. He did not care about the moat or the boat. He wanted to eat. He yelled down the hole, "I want to eat! Do you have some roast beef on toast?" This time, Mole was more bold. He told that old goat, "All right, have half a loaf, but don't choke!"

Goat told Mole, "You are a very good host!"

After lunch, Mole went for a float on his boat in the moat.

Mole

After reading "Mole," answer the following questions.

1. What is the main idea of the story?

    A. Mole was not bold. He was shy.

    B. Toad was not bold. He was shy.

    C. Goat was not bold. He was shy.

2. Why didn't Mole want Toad to know about his boat?

    A. Toad would hide in the boat.

    B. Toad would soak his boat.

    C. Toad would mope in the boat.

3. What did Goat want from Mole?

    A. roast beef on toast

    B. gold

    C. to play

4. What is another word for *poked*?

    A. stopped

    B. floated

    C. jabbed

5. What is the meaning of the word *host* in this story?

    A. someone who takes care of a guest

    B. a place for another animal to live

    C. a large number

6. Write the long *o* words in the right group.

hope   boat   froze

note   road   moat

roast   choke

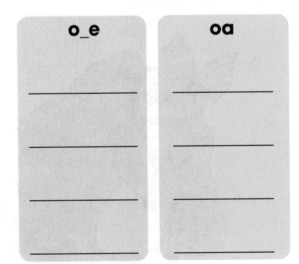

o_e	oa
_____	_____
_____	_____
_____	_____
_____	_____

Duke and Mule

Read the poem below.

Duke was a dude who lived in the city.

He visited a ranch.

He tried to ride a mule.

The mule was rude.

It did not move.

Duke was not happy.

He sang a tune.

The mule did not like it.

Duke fed the mule.

He gave it a sugar cube.

The mule was happy.

It gave Duke a ride.

54

Duke and Mule

After reading "Duke and Mule," answer the following questions.

1. What did Duke want to do?
   A. sing a song
   B. rope a horse
   C. ride a mule
   D. feed a cow

2. What did the mule not like?
   A. Duke's song
   B. sugar
   C. hay
   D. work

3. Why did the mule give Duke a ride?
   A. Duke gave the mule a carrot.
   B. Duke gave the mule a sugar cube.
   C. Duke gave the mule an apple.
   D. Duke gave the mule water.

4. What did the mule do when Duke tried to ride him?
   A. It trotted away.
   B. It lay down.
   C. It ran away.
   D. It did not move.

5. Who was Duke?
   A. a dancer
   B. a farmer
   C. a dude who lived in the city

6. Write the six u_e words from the story.

   _____

   _____

   _____

   _____

   _____

   _____

Summer Bridge Reading RB-904091

Long Vowel Sounds

When a vowel sounds like its name, it makes a long vowel sound.
Example: *a* in *take*, *i* in *like*

Add the beginning sound and the vowel sound to finish writing each word.

1.

___ ___ v e

2.

___ ___ k e

3.

___ ___ n e

4.

___ ___ m e

5.

___ ___ l

6.
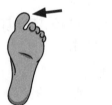
___ ___ e

7.

___ ___ k e

8.

___ ___ t e

9.

___ ___ r e

The Shipmate

Read the story below. Then, answer the questions.

James' Uncle Nate has a sailboat. The name of Nate's boat is *Ride the Wind*. James is Uncle Nate's shipmate. James keeps the boat clean and neat. He washes the deck with soap and water. He beats the sails with brushes and brooms. He checks for rust.

Uncle Nate and James keep track of the weather. They listen for the weather forecast so that they will know when it is safe to take the boat on the water. They like to fish in their spare time. James always checks to see if the fishing poles they use are clean and strong.

One day, James and Uncle Nate catch a big wave. Out they sail! The sky is blue. Nate raves about the perfect day they are having. Then, it starts to rain.

The lake is no longer safe. The wind seems to scream, "You had better race to shore!" James is brave as he helps his Uncle Nate sail the boat back to shore. Uncle Nate hugs James. He says, "You are the best shipmate I have ever had. You are a keeper."

1. Who are the main characters in the story?_____

2. Where are James and Uncle Nate? _____

3. Unscramble the words. Then, write them under the correct vowels. The words are in the story if you need help .

wokn	teaN	obta	imte	erkpree
mJsae	aetn	edir	elub	seu
Long a	Long e	Long i	Long o	Long u

_____ _____ _____ _____ _____

_____ _____ _____ _____ _____

4. What did Uncle Nate mean when he told James, "You are a keeper"?

_____

Summer Bridge Reading RB-904091

Dawn the Zookeeper

Read the story below.

Dawn is a zookeeper. Her job is to keep the animals in the zoo safe and happy. She cleans the cages and gives the animals clean straw. Last week, a hawk began to squawk. Dawn saw that it had a sore claw. She called a vet to fix the hawk's claw. Another time, two of the big cats got in a brawl over raw meat. One cat got a hurt paw. The other cat had a sore jaw. Dawn took care of the big cats. Dawn loves animals. Dawn loves her job.

Dawn the Zookeeper

After reading "Dawn the Zookeeper," answer the following questions.

1. Which sentence tells the main idea of the story?

   A. Dawn takes care of the animals at the zoo.

   B. Dawn is safe and happy.

   C. The animals like Dawn.

2. What is a zookeeper's job?

   A. to only play with the animals

   B. to only feed the animals

   C. to keep the animals safe and happy

3. What happened to the hawk?

   A. It had a sore claw.

   B. It was hungry.

   C. It couldn't fly.

4. What happened to the big cats?

   A. They wanted water.

   B. They got in a brawl.

   C. They didn't like each other.

5. What does *brawl* mean?

   A. cage

   B. fight

   C. game

6. Write eight *aw* words from the story.

_____

_____

_____

_____

_____

_____

_____

_____

59

It's Cold Outside

A **cause** is what makes something happen.

An **effect** is the thing that happens.

Read each pair of sentences. Write *C* in front of the sentence that tells about the cause. Write *E* in front of the sentence that tells about the effect.

1. _____ It was cold outside.

   _____ Tom started shivering.

2. _____ That made his hands warm.

   _____ He rubbed his hands together.

3. _____ That made his hands much warmer.

   _____ Tom put his mittens on.

60

It's Cold Outside

> A **cause** is what makes something happen.
>
> An **effect** is the thing that happens.

Use your imagination to write an effect for each cause.

1. Susie jumps in
a puddle.

_____

_____

2. Ian forgets to do
his homework.

_____

_____

3. Nan leaves a
book outside.

_____

_____

4. Andrew hugs
his sister.

_____

_____

61

Read the poem below.

When the cat fell in the pool, the Zoo Crew knew what to do.
They threw a loop.

When the goose threw a broom, the Zoo Crew knew what to do.
They ducked!

When the giraffe blew his nose, the Zoo Crew knew what to do.
They stood back!

When the hen flew the coop, the Zoo Crew knew what to do.
They took a break.

When the cow jumped over the moon, the Zoo Crew knew what to do.
They laughed.

The Zoo Crew

After reading "The Zoo Crew," answer the following questions.

1. Who are the characters in the story?

_____

_____

_____

2. Draw a line between each problem and its solution.

cat fell in the pool	they ducked
goose threw a broom	they laughed
hen flew the coop	they threw a loop
cow jumped over the moon	they took a break

3. Find three words from the story for each group.

ew words	*oo* words
_____	_____
_____	_____
_____	_____

4. A coop is a home for what kind of animal?

A. cat
B. cow
C. giraffe
D. hen

5. What is another word for *coop*?

A. box
B. house
C. door

63

Be a Word Detective

> When you read a word that you do not know, sometimes you can find the meaning from clues in the sentence.
> **Example:** The boy *giggled* at the funny story.
> The word *funny* gives you a clue about the meaning of *giggled*.
> *Giggle* means to laugh.

Use clues in each sentence to find which word should go in the blank.
Circle the correct words.

1. I use _____ to clean.
   fast   soap   time

2. The _____ hopped in the grass.
   rabbit   doll   car

3. We planted _____ in the garden.
   ducks   boys   seeds

4. There is a _____ in the sky.
   door   cloud   tree

5. We rode our _____ to the park.
   bikes   house   ball

6. You must _____ your room.
   jump   sleep   clean

7. She went to a friend's _____.
   party   bath   plant

8. The cat is _____ the basket.
   sing   blow   under

Summer Bridge Reading RB-904091

Figuring It Out

Circle the best meaning for each bold word.

1. The noisy **locomotive** drove into the station on the tracks.

   car   train   dog

2. Ginny was **elated** to find her lost kitten.

   upset   scared   happy

3. "I don't like spinach," **grumbled** Gabriel.

   smiled   yelled   said with a frown

4. Mrs. Twerkle **admired** the beautiful dress that Janet wore to the party.

   liked   danced   tore up

5. Ms. Sally will **donate** many books to the library.

   steal   give   write in

6. My brother and I come to this park **frequently**.

   for free   often   listen to the radio

Troy and the Gold Coin

Read the story below.

A long time ago, there lived a boy named Troy. Troy dreamed of becoming a knight. The king held a royal competition each year to find the kindest person in the kingdom. The winner each year became a knight and won a prize. Troy entered the competition. While Troy was waiting for his turn, he discovered a gold coin wrapped in foil on the floor. He picked it up and looked around to find the owner. Nobody appeared to be missing anything, so he placed it in his pocket.

When it was his turn to meet the king, the king looked sad. Troy asked him why he looked so sad. The king said he had lost the prize for the competition. Troy pulled the gold coin from his pocket and offered it to the king. The king was so impressed with Troy's kindness that he made him a knight.

Summer Bridge Reading RB-904091

Troy and the Gold Coin

After reading "Troy and the Gold Coin," answer the following questions.

1. What could be another title for this story?
   - **A.** The King Is a Hero
   - **B.** Troy Becomes a Knight
   - **C.** Knights Unite

2. What did Troy want?
   - **A.** to become a knight
   - **B.** a gold coin
   - **C.** to eat lunch

3. What did the king want?
   - **A.** to find the kindest person in the kingdom
   - **B.** to find a jester
   - **C.** to build a new castle

4. How did Troy become a knight?
   - **A.** He offered the coin he found to the king.
   - **B.** He cried.
   - **C.** He saved a princess.

5. Put the words in the correct groups.

   boy   Troy   foil
   royal   coil   coin

oi words	*oy* words
_____	_____
_____	_____
_____	_____

6. What does *kindness* mean?
   - **A.** to be kind
   - **B.** to be mean
   - **C.** to save

© Rainbow Bridge Publishing   **Summer Bridge Reading** RB-904091

Who Are the Characters?

A **character** is a person or animal in a story.
Example: Scott rode the whale across the sea.
Scott and the whale are the characters.

Read the summary of *Arthur Goes to Camp* by Marc Brown (Little, Brown and Company, 1982). Underline the characters. Then, circle the characters in the word find below. Names will go across and down.

Arthur and his friends the Brain, Buster, and Francine left for Camp Meadowcroak. They rode in a bus. Muffy went to the camp, too. She rode there in a limo. Becky was the girls' camp leader. Rocky was the boys' camp leader. Arthur helped his team win the scavenger hunt.

Brain   Buster   Francine   Arthur   Muffy   Rocky   Becky

L	M	A	F	R	A	N	C	I	N	E
B	U	S	T	E	R	B	N	E	I	T
E	F	C	P	Q	T	R	O	C	K	Y
C	F	R	D	G	H	M	Z	Y	K	O
K	Y	B	R	A	U	M	U	W	F	R
Y	V	E	B	B	R	A	I	N	X	J

"Setting" the Stage

> The **setting** tells where and when a story takes place. To find what a story's setting is, read the sentences carefully and look for clues.

Read each passage. Then, answer each question.

Tony plays by a body of water. There are ducks swimming in the water. Many trees grow near the water.

1. Where is Tony playing?
   - **A.** near a pond
   - **B.** by the ocean
   - **C.** at a school
   - **D.** in his house

There is a busy street near Carly's house. Many cars drive on the street. There is a bus stop in front of her house.

2. Where does Carly live?
   - **A.** at the beach
   - **B.** in the country
   - **C.** by a river
   - **D.** in the city

Kristen's family has many animals. A fence is in front of her house. A barn is next to her house.

3. Where does Kristen live?
   - **A.** next to a church
   - **B.** a farm
   - **C.** in a log cabin
   - **D.** in an apartment

Story Clues

Read the story. Read the sentences. Circle the sentence that is true.

You can plant a sunflower in your yard. In the spring, the dirt is soft and warm. Poke a hole in the dirt for your seed. Drop it in and cover it up.

Soon, roots and little leaves will grow. In the summer, your plant will grow a huge flower.

In the fall, your plant will die. Some of the seeds will fall out of the flower. They will land in the dirt. They will stay in the ground until spring. Then, they will grow into new sunflower plants.

A sunflower plant lives more than 10 years.

Sunflower plants live only one year.

Sunflowers bloom in the winter.

Read the story. Then, answer the question.

Tom has many pets. He keeps them in a jar. The jar is full of dirt. He feeds his pets drops of honey.

His pets dig rooms in the dirt. Tom likes to see them work. He will put them back outside soon.

His pets are not tame. They are wild.

What are Tom's pets?

dogs   ants   ponies

Story Clues

Read each passage. Then, circle the best answer to the question.

Sue Lee rode to the store. She rode up a big hill. She had to pedal hard. It was easy to ride down the other side. Sue Lee went very fast. She had to use her brakes.

1. What did Sue Lee ride?

a horse   a skateboard   a bike

Sam likes to swing the bat and hit the ball. He loves to run to first base. Sometimes, he even makes it to third base. He wants to play shortstop when he grows up.

2. What game does Sam like?

football   baseball   golf

Summer Bridge Reading RB-904091

Our Tree House

Read the poem below.

My friend and I are way up high,
watching as the world goes by
from our tree house.
Down below on the ground,
little people move around
below our tree house.
Birds fly above and below us.
They screech and make a fuss
around our tree house.

Our Tree House

After reading "Our Tree House," answer the following questions.

1. Which sentence tells the main idea of the poem?
   - A. People on the ground are little.
   - B. Birds fly in the sky.
   - C. It is fun to play in a tree house.

2. What two people are in the tree house?
   - A. a boy and a girl
   - B. my friend and I
   - C. two boys

3. How do the people on the ground look from the tree house?
   - A. like big people
   - B. like little people
   - C. like giants

4. Why are the people little?
   - A. They are children.
   - B. They are short.
   - C. They look little from up high.

5. Write three *ou* words from the poem.

   _____

   _____

   _____

6. What does *screech* mean?
   - A. to circle around
   - B. to make a loud sound
   - C. to fly around

To the Moon

A **fact** is something that you know is true.
An **opinion** is what you believe about something.
Example: Mr. Greene is a teacher. (This is a fact.)
Mr. Greene is the best teacher. (This is an opinion.)

Get the rocket to the moon. Color the stars that tell a fact blue.

Earth is a planet.

It is fun to ride in a rocket.

Earth has a moon.

The sun is the best star.

Stars are interesting.

There are many stars in the sky.

Earth is the greatest planet.

Stars are beautiful.

The sun gives Earth light.

74

Thunder and Lightning

Read the passage below.

The sky lights up with a flash. "Crash!" Thunder booms. Lightning is a very big electric spark. Thunder is the noise made by lightning.

Lightning happens during a storm. The clouds fill with an electric charge. The electricity in the clouds moves quickly to the ground. The path of the electricity is a bright streak of light. It is called *lightning*.

Lightning moves faster than its sound. When lightning is close, you hear the thunder at the same time. When lightning is far away, you hear the thunder later. When you see lightning, count the seconds until you hear the thunder. If you count 5 seconds, the lightning is one mile away. If you count 10 seconds, the lightning is two miles away.

Lightning can be very dangerous. When a storm begins, you should go inside. You will be much safer inside.

Circle *fact* or *opinion* after each statement.

1.	Lightning is dangerous.	fact	opinion
2.	Lightning is scary.	fact	opinion
3.	Thunder is too loud.	fact	opinion
4.	Thunder is the noise that lightning makes.	fact	opinion
5.	Inside, you are safer during a storm.	fact	opinion
6.	Dark clouds are beautiful.	fact	opinion

Where Do They Go?

Look at the pictures at the bottom of the page. Write the name of each creature under the correct column.

Two Legs	Four Legs	Six Legs

What Can You Find?

Look around your home or classroom. Write what you see that fits each description. Can you find . . .

something red?

_____

something colorful?

_____

something made of wood?

_____

something shiny?

_____

something that should be outside?

_____

something soft?

_____

something smaller than your hand?

_____

something bigger than you?

_____

something older than you?

_____

something younger than you?

_____

something with holes in it?

_____

something noisy?

_____

something that smells good?

_____

something that tastes good?

_____

something that belongs somewhere else?

_____

Summer Bridge Reading RB-904091

World of Color

Read the poem below.

Look for colors all around.

Everywhere colors can be found.

Green is for grass and fresh peas.

Brown is for bears and trunks of trees.

Red is for roses and valentine hearts.

Black are the words on white reading charts.

Blue are the birds in the blue sky.

Orange is for oranges, don't ask me why.

Yellow is for bananas, apples, and pears.

Colors, all colors, for rocket flares.

Purple cows, I don't think so.

Are pigs pink? I don't really know.

Colorful rainbows can be found.

Look, there are colors all around.

World of Color

After reading "World of Color," answer the following questions.

1. Write one more thing for each color listed below.

Green: grass, fresh peas, _____

Brown: bears, trunks of trees,_____

Red: roses, valentine hearts,_____

Black: words, _____

White: charts, _____

Blue: birds, sky,_____

Orange: oranges,_____

Yellow: bananas, apples, pears, _____

2. Find and write the words in the poem that fit each description listed below:

    A. contraction _____

    B. two long *i* words with no letter *i* _____

    C. three words with the *ow, ou* sound _____

    D. a compound word _____

3. Write the base or root word for the following words.

colorful _____   reading _____

really _____   roses _____

Monkeying Around

Read each paragraph. Then, write a sentence to tell what you think might happen next.

Morgan the monkey wanted to play. She climbed a tree looking for her friend Mabel. "Mabel is not here," Mabel's mom said. "She is playing with Mombo by the river."

1. What will Morgan do? _____

_____

_____

The three monkeys played by the river. They liked to run and chase each other. Mombo was the fastest. He always caught Mabel and Morgan. They decided to have a race.

2. Who will win? _____

_____

_____

Morgan, Mabel, and Mombo were tired from running. They all liked to take a nap in the afternoon. The three monkeys climbed a tree. They swung from tree to tree back home.

3. What will the monkeys do next? _____

_____

_____

What Will Happen?

Read each passage. Read the three endings. Choose the ending that makes the most sense.

1. Jade's class was going on a trip. They were going to the zoo. A big bus came to get them.
   - **A.** They all went home.
   - **B.** They got on the bus.
   - **C.** They went out to play.

2. They rode for a long time. Then, the bus came to a stop. They were at the zoo!
   - **A.** They all got off.
   - **B.** They went to the store.
   - **C.** They got up on top of the bus.

3. They went into the zoo. They went to see the lion. He had a big mane. He had big teeth.
   - **A.** He ate a car.
   - **B.** He was not there.
   - **C.** He had a big roar.

81

Tanner and Andy's Clubhouse

Directions are steps for doing something. Always be sure to do each step in order. Do not skip any steps. Pay attention to key words, such as number words and color words.

Help Tanner and Andy finish building their clubhouse. Follow each step in order.

1. Draw the outline of a house.
2. Draw two square windows.
3. Write *Clubhouse* above the door.
4. Draw a rectangle around the word *Clubhouse*.
5. Color the clubhouse brown.
6. Color the door red.
7. Draw a roof.
8. Color the roof green.
9. Draw yourself near the clubhouse.

Summer Bridge Reading RB-904091

© Rainbow Bridge Publishing

Worms in Dirt

Draw the steps for making worms in dirt. Show each ingredient clearly.

Ingredients:
2 small boxes of instant
   chocolate pudding
3½ cups (840 ml) milk
1 small tub of whipped topping
10 chocolate sandwich cookies
1 bag of gummy worms
8 clear plastic cups

Directions:
1. In a large bowl, mix pudding and milk until smooth.

2. Stir in the whipped topping.

3. Put the chocolate cookies in a sealed plastic bag. Crush the cookies by rolling them in the bag with a rolling pin.

4. Put a little pudding in each cup. Put some cookie crumbs on the pudding.

5. Add a little more pudding and sprinkle the rest of the cookie crumbs over the top.

6. Put two gummy worms in each cup.

1.	2.	3.
4.	5.	6.

Could It Happen?

> Some stories are about things that can really happen. These are
> **reality** stories. Some stories are about things that could not really
> happen. These are **fantasy** stories.
> **Example:** The mouse ran under the chair. (reality)
> The mouse rode a bike. (fantasy)

Circle the sentences that tell about something that could really happen.
Draw a square around the sentences that tell about something that
could not really happen.

1. The boy flew across the ocean on a magic carpet.

2. Caleb built a castle in the sand.

3. The turtle put its head in its shell.

4. The fish read a book about birds.

5. The crab crawled across the sand.

6. The cow drove the tractor.

84

Could It Happen?

Read each paragraph. Decide whether it is reality or fantasy. Circle the correct word. Draw a picture of the events in the paragraph.

1. Alexander splashed in the fluffy cloud pool. He jumped from cloud to cloud, throwing shooting stars and raindrops into the air. Down below, it started to rain and thunder.

reality  fantasy

2. Tamika was playing dress up. She dressed up in a sparkly gold dress. She put on fancy play shoes. Then, she walked into a castle. There was a king and a queen at the ball. She was Cinderella.

reality  fantasy

3. Shannon pushed the crying baby in the stroller. They walked around the block several times. Shannon sang songs while they walked. After an hour, the baby fell asleep.

reality fantasy

Summer Bridge Reading RB-904091

Moving On

Read the story below.

I packed my toys. I put my clothes in a box. My books were coming, too. I said good-bye to my room. I said good-bye to my swing set. I said good-bye to my friend. I did not want to go.

My new house is big. I have my own room. I hope my mom remembered my bike. There are kids next door. I wonder if they know how to play hide-and-seek. I am glad to be here.

Draw a picture of the child at the old house and at the new house. Show what the child does at each house.

1. What do you think is bad about moving?

_____

2. What do you think is good about moving?

_____

Sisters

Read the story below.

My big sister loves to talk. She talks about what she sees and does. She reads books when she is not talking. She talks about what she reads. She reads about people, animals, and places. I like to listen to her. I am quiet. I like to close my eyes and imagine pictures in my head. I can imagine the things my sister talks about. I like to draw pictures, too. My sister likes to look at my pictures. She thinks I am smart. I think she is smart.

Copy words from the word bank into the Venn diagram.

Big Sister   **Little Sister**

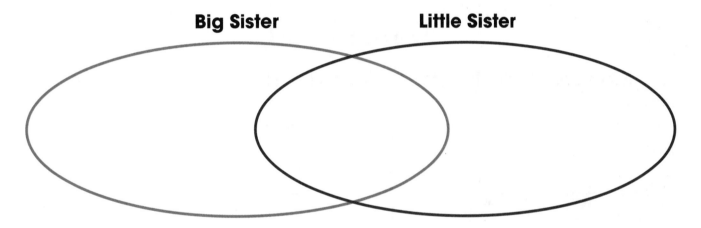

Word Bank

quiet	talkative	likes to read
likes to draw	listens	thinks her sister is smart

1. Which sister is more like you?_____

2. What do you like to do best? _____

Summer Bridge Reading RB-904091

What's the Title?

The first page of a book is usually the **title page**. It tells the title of the book, who wrote the book (the author), and who made the pictures (the illustrator).

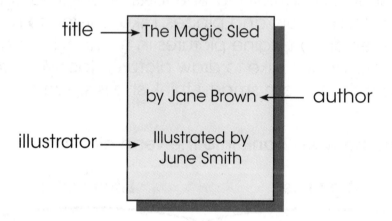

Find two books. Write the title, author, and illustrator of each book on the title pages below.

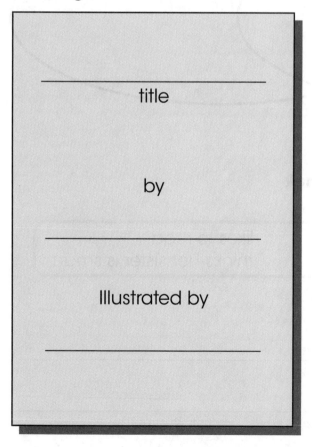

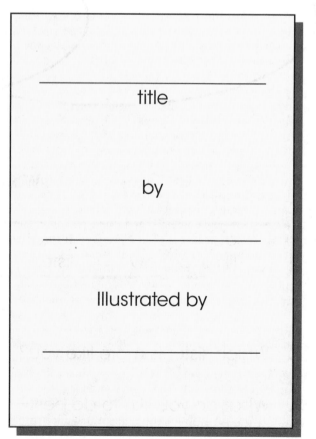

Summer Bridge Reading RB-904091

Bats

Most chapter books and longer informational books have a **table of contents** after the title page. The table of contents tells the beginning page number for the chapters or topics in the book.

Table of Contents

Use the table of contents above to answer the questions.

1. The title of Chapter 2 is _____.

2. Chapter _____ begins on page 15.

3. How many chapters are in the book? _____

4. Chapter _____ would tell you about brown bats.

5. Bats have thumbs on their wings. Chapter _____ would tell you this fact.

6. Chapter _____ will tell you what bats eat.

7. What chapter will tell you where bats live? _____

Summer Bridge Reading RB-904091

What's the Plot?

The **plot** is what happens in a story. A character in a story often must solve a problem. The problem and how the character solves the problem are part of the plot.

Read each passage below. Then, answer the questions.

Maddie and her family went to the park for a picnic. They put a big blanket on the ground. Maddie's mom set the picnic basket on the blanket. Then, they went for a walk. When they returned there were hundreds of ants on the blanket. Maddie's dad grabbed the picnic basket. The family moved to a picnic table to enjoy their lunch.

1. What was the problem? _____

    _____

2. How did Maddie's family solve the problem? _____

    _____

It was the day of the big race at Jackson's school. Jackson was excited about the race. He was a fast runner. He ran even faster when he wore his black tennis shoes. After breakfast, he went to his room to put on his black shoes. The shoes were not there. Where could they be? Jackson decided to ask everyone in his family if they had seen his shoes. He found his younger brother, Alex, wearing his shoes. Alex wanted to run fast, too.

3. What was the problem? _____

    _____

4. How did Jackson solve the problem? _____

    _____

A Day in the Garden

> **Character traits** are the ways a character looks, acts, or feels. You learn about character traits through details in the sentences of a story.

Sara and her friends worked in the garden. Sara wore a hat over her curly hair. Kip was very happy. He liked planting seeds. He wore his favorite shirt with lots of stars on it. Ali was tired and hot. She did not like working in the garden. Her sandals hurt her feet. Jack wore two different socks. He did not help. He played in the dirt.

Write the name of each character next to the correct picture.

1. _____

2. _____

3. _____

4. _____

Summer Bridge Reading RB-904091

Become a Writer

You have learned about the characters, setting, and plot of stories. They are called the story's **elements**. Now, put it all together.

Follow the steps below and on page 93 to plan a story.

1. Plan two characters. Write their names and two words to describe each.

   1. _____

      A. _____

      B. _____

   2. _____

      A. _____

      B. _____

2. Where will your story take place? Write about your setting.

   _____

   _____

3. Draw a picture of your setting below.

4. Plan the beginning, middle, and end of your story.

Beginning

_____

_____

_____

_____

Middle

_____

_____

_____

_____

End

_____

_____

_____

_____

5. Turn your plan into a story or book! Use paper and pencil or a computer. Then, share your story with a friend.

Summer Bridge Reading RB-904091

Answer Key

Page 10
1. cat, hat, bat, sat;
2. Max; 3. cap, hat, bag, bat;
4. Answers will vary.;
5. Answers will vary.;
6. Picture should show Sam and Max.

Page 11
1. farm animals; 2. things that go; 3. food; 4. pets;
5. tools; 6. shapes

Page 13
1. B.; 2. T, T, F, T, F, F, T; 3. B.;
4. A.; 5. Big pets: horse, sheep, cow; Little pets: gerbil, hamster, mouse;
6. Meg, Vet, pets, help, get, well, leg, mend, pep

Page 14
1. My Pet Fish; 2. A Trip to the Moon; 3. Fun at the Pool; 4. A Bird Adventure;
5. I'm All Wet!; 6. The Cat Picture; 7. Answers will vary.

Page 15
1. Ducks Are Made for Water; 2. How Ducks Stay Warm

Page 17
1. A.; 2. fish, dish; ship, trip; chip, dip; pig, jig; 3. A.; 4. Y, Y, Y, N; 5. Answers will vary.

Page 18
1. meat; 2. plants; 3. plates;
4. horns; 5. necks; 6. short;
7. eggs

Page 19

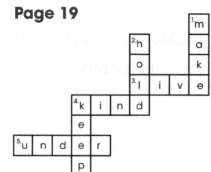

Page 21
1. B.; 2. T, F, T, F; 3. A.; 4. A. man, B. gold, C. pots; 5. A.;
6. A.

Page 22
3, 2, 4, 1; Extra: Answers will vary.

Page 23
1. 2, 3, 1; 2. 2, 1, 3; 3. 3, 2, 1;
4. 2, 3, 1

Page 25
1. B.; 2. 4, 2, 1, 3, 5; 3. B.;
4. Answers will vary.; 5. B.

Page 26
1. cap; 2. place; 3. quick;
4. keep; 5. kind; 6. sleep;
7. run; 8. choose

Page 27
1. day, night; 2. long, short;
3. big, little; 4. hot, cold;
5. old, new; 6. over, under

Page 28
1. cup; 2. dot; 3. leg; 4. fan;
5. mop; 6. lips; 7. pig; 8. net;
9. hat; 10. truck

Page 30
1. A.; 2. Bigger than a dog: yak, pig, ram; Smaller than a dog: cat, ant, rat, hen; 3. Answers will vary.;
4. whispered, barked, buzzed

Page 31
1. Wheels make things easy to move.; 2. People had to move things without wheels.

Page 33
1. C.; 2. B.; 3. A.; 4. baby, Dad, Grandpa, sister;
5. Answers will vary.;
6. napping, snoozing

Page 34
Something to Eat: apples, cheese, beans, bread; Something to Wear: shirt, pants, gloves, cap; A Place to Live: cave, cabin, lodge, tent

Page 35
1. dog; 2. car; 3. toys; 4. girl;
5. paper; 6. sit

Page 37
1. B.; 2. C.; 3. B.; 4. C.; 5. Toy: choo choo train, chopper toy, checkers; Not a Toy: chestnut, chair, chocolate;
6. thing, bring; chain, rain; air, chair

Summer Bridge Reading RB-904091 © Rainbow Bridge Publishing

Answer Key

Page 38

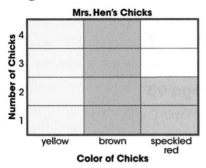

Mrs. Hen's Chicks

Page 39

Pictures will vary.; 1. jobs;
2. sand; 3. babies;
4. baby ants

Page 40

1. child; 2. whale; 3. catch;
4. ship; 5. wish; 6. thumb

```
c  (w  i  s  h)  l  (c
(t  h  u  m  b)  k   h
(c  a  t  c  h)  s   i
 e   l  m  f  a  n   l
 d  (e)(s  h  i  p)  d)
```

Page 41

1. C.; 2. B.

Page 43

1. A; 2. Answers will vary.;
3. Answers will vary.;
4. math, path; out, about;
thread, head; 5. *th* sound
in *thin*: things, math, think;
th sound in *then*: this, that,
there

Page 45

1. B; 2. Answers will vary.;
3. A; 4. Answers will vary.;
5. Answers will vary.

Page 47

1. B.; 2. 4, 1, 2, 3; 3. A.;
4. Answers will vary.; 5. a_e:
snake, cake, same, race;
ay: Gayle, day, play, Jay;
ai: sail, tail, train, trail

Page 49

1. Answers will vary.;
2. Answers will vary.; 3. out,
go, there, best, young/new,
me, up, go, good

Page 50

1. funny; 2. afraid; 3. nice;
4. proud; 5. tired; 6. sad

Page 51

1. A.; 2. C.; 3. A.

Page 53

1. A.; 2. B.; 3. A.; 4. C.; 5. A.;
6. o_e: choke, froze, hope,
note; oa: boat, moat,
road, roast

Page 55

1. C.; 2. A.; 3. B.; 4. D.; 5. C.;
6. Duke, dude, mule, rude,
tune, cube

Page 56

1. wave; 2. bike; 3. bone;
4. home; 5. eel; 6. toe;
7. cake; 8. kite; 9. tire

Page 57

1. Uncle Nate, James; 2. a
boat on a lake; 3. Long *a*:
James, Nate; Long *e*: neat,
keeper; Long *i*: ride, time;
Long *o*: boat, know; Long
u: blue, use; 4. James did a
good job, and Uncle Nate
appreciated it.

Page 59

1. A.; 2. C.; 3. A.; 4. B.; 5. B.;
6. Dawn, straw, hawk,
squawk, saw, claw, brawl,
jaw, raw, paw

Page 60

1. C, E; 2. E, C; 3. E, C

Page 61

Answers will vary.

Page 63

1. Zoo Crew, cat, goose,
giraffe, hen, cow; 2. cat
fell in the pool, they threw
a loop; goose threw a
broom, they ducked; hen
flew the coop, they took a
break; cow jumped over
the moon, they laughed;
3. Answers will vary.; 4. D.;
5. B.

Page 64

1. soap; 2. rabbit; 3. seeds;
4. cloud; 5. bikes; 6. clean;
7. party; 8. under

Page 65

1. train; 2. happy; 3. said
with a frown; 4. liked; 5. give;
6. often

Page 67

1. B.; 2. A.; 3. A.; 4. A.; 5. oi
words: coin, foil, coil; *oy*
words: boy, Troy, royal; 6. A.

Page 68

```
L  (M  A  (F  R  A  N  C  I  N  E)
(B  U  S  T  E  R)  B  N  E  I  T
E   F  C  P  Q  T  (R  O  C  K  Y)
C  (F)  R  D  G  H  M  Z  Y  K  O
K  (Y)  B  R  A  U  M  U  W  F  R
Y)  V  E  B  (B  R  A  I  N)  X  J
```

Summer Bridge Reading RB-904091

Answer Key

Page 69
1. A.; 2. D.; 3. B.

Page 70
Sunflower plants live only one year; ants

Page 71
1. a bike; 2. baseball

Page 73
1. C.; 2. B.; 3. B.; 4. C.; 5. our, ground, around, house; 6. B.

Page 74
Earth is a planet.; Earth has a moon.; There are many stars in the sky.; The sun gives Earth light.

Page 75
1. fact; 2. opinion; 3. opinion; 4. fact; 5. fact; 6. opinion

Page 76
Two Legs: man, bird; Four Legs: horse, dog; Six Legs: ant, ladybug

Page 77
Answers will vary.

Page 79
1. Answers will vary.;
2. A. don't; B. why, sky; C. brown, found, cows, around; D. rainbows;
3. from right to left and top to bottom: color, read, real, rose

Page 80
Answers will vary.

Page 81
1. B.; 2. A.; 3. C.

Page 82
The final picture should follow directions.

Page 83
The final pictures should follow directions.

Page 84
1. fantasy; 2. reality; 3. reality; 4. fantasy; 5. reality; 6. fantasy

Page 85
1. fantasy; 2. fantasy; 3. reality

Page 86
Answers will vary.

Page 87
Answers will vary.

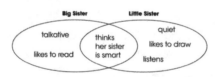

Page 88
Answers will vary.

Page 89
1. A Bat's Wings; 2. 4; 3. 4; 4. 1; 5. 2; 6. 3; 7. 4

Page 90
1. Hundreds of ants were on their picnic blanket.;
2. The family moved to a picnic table to eat.;
3. Jackson could not find his running shoes.; 4. He asked his family if they had seen his shoes.

Page 91
1. Jack; 2. Ali; 3. Kip; 4. Sara

Page 92
Answers will vary.

Page 93
Answers will vary.

Summer Bridge Reading RB-904091